Finding the Right One

An Interactive Workbook for Individuals and Groups

JIMMY EVANS AND FRANK MARTIN

Finding the Right One

Interactive Workbook for Individuals or Groups
Jimmy Evans and Frank Martin

How to Use This Study 5

Introduction 9

Session One: *Searching for a "Soul Mate"* 11

Session Two: *Exposing the Myths of Love* 17

Session Three: *Healthy and Realistic Expectations* 25

Session Four: *The Right (and Wrong) Way to Date* 35

Session Five: *Recognizing Red Flags* 43

Session Six: *Developing a Spirit of Compatibility* 53

Session Seven: *Purposeful Conversations* 63

Session Eight: *The Power of Covenant* 71

Suggestions for Leaders 79

Endnotes 85

Pre-Marriage Inventory 87

How to Use This Study

Welcome to *Finding the Right One*, an interactive study guide for individuals or groups. If you are single, and hope to someday find yourself in a committed, fulfilling marriage relationship, you've come to the right place. This study was designed specifically with you in mind!

To get the most out of this study, we encourage you to use it as a companion to our book, *The Right One*. Many of the ideas and principles we address here are developed in more detail in the book, so if you take time to read that first, you'll be further ahead of the game. It's not a prerequisite, but a good suggestion. We've designed this workbook to be used as a stand-alone study, so whether you are going through it alone or in a small group setting, you should have all you need for an engaging and in-depth study.

Included with this workbook is a teaching DVD developed by Jimmy Evans and the *Marriage Today* team. These DVD lessons contain thoughts and ideas that are not necessarily included in the book or workbook, and they will add a great deal to your study, so it's important to watch them for further insight. Whether going through this study alone, or in a group setting, we encourage you to have a DVD player on hand to take advantage of this added resource.

Who Will Benefit From This Study?

Simply put, anyone who is single and hoping to someday marry the person that God has in mind for them will gain a great deal of wisdom and understanding from this eight-week series. It is designed as a small group resource for high school, college, or singles ministries, but it can also be used by individuals for private study and reflection.

Engaged couples can also benefit, since many of the included thoughts and questions lead to conversations that pre-married people need to be having. If you are engaged, or in a serious dating relationship, you are heading toward one of the most critical decisions of your life, and you want to move forward with your eyes wide open. This series is designed to help you do just that.

Suggestions for Individual Study

We encourage you to begin each new session in prayer, asking God to give you wisdom as you seek his will for your future.

Take time to watch the corresponding DVD lesson at the beginning of each new session.

After reading through the opening thoughts from the day's lesson, don't forget to read the suggested Bible passage. Read it slowly, and meditate on the words before moving onto the lesson. Pray for any specific insight or instruction God may have for you as you go through the day's lesson.

Write out your answers to each question, just as you would if you were preparing for a group study. It my be tempting to skip over this part and simply meditate on your answers, but writing them out will help you process your thoughts much more clearly. It will also allow this workbook to serve as something of a journal for future reference.

End each lesson in final prayer and reflection, asking God to help you incorporate the lessons learned into your daily life. If any particular thought or concept has stood out to you, make a mental note to keep it in your prayers as you go about your day.

Suggestions for Group Study

Try to come to each session prepared. You'll get more out of the study if you take time to read through each lesson and answer the questions ahead of time.

As you watch the corresponding DVD lessons, pay close attention, and take notes of any thoughts or ideas you'd like to discuss further once the discussion has begun.

Come ready to participate. A group study is not a lecture, and you'll get more out of the lesson if you're willing to involve yourself in the conversation.

Steer clear of "rabbit trails." In a group discussion, it's often tempting to bring up other books or commentaries you've read, or a documentary you once saw, but that can easily derail the conversation. Try to focus on the question or passage at hand, and it will be much easier for the leader to keep the study on topic.

Listen when others speak, and try not to dominate the discussion. Our personalities often drive how we react during a group discussion, and it's easy for extroverts to unwittingly take over. Keep your comments brief and pertinent, and leave room for everyone to participate.

If you are the discussion leader, remember to start on time and end on time. And do your preparation ahead of time, so that everyone in the group can get the most out of each lesson. We've included a "Leader's Guide" at the back of this book to help you do that.

The Right One

Introduction

I (Frank) still remember the first time I saw my wife Ruthie. I was twenty-five at the time, and attending a citywide lecture event at my former college. I was standing in the floor of the school coliseum, visiting with a group of friends, and I turned just in time to see her walking toward us. She was smiling and holding hands with a guy I had never seen.

Apparently, one of my friends knew him, because the two of them walked up and immediately joined our conversation. I waited for someone to introduce me, but no one did, so I stood to one side thinking, *Who is that beautiful girl, and why is she holding hands with that pinhead?*

After a few minutes, the two of them went on their way. To this day, Ruthie says she doesn't remember that conversation (which shows how much of an impression I made), but I've never forgotten it.

By happenstance, I saw her again just a few weeks later at a small group Bible study. This time

> "Finding the right marriage partner is the second most important decision any of us will ever make, trumped only by our decision to become followers of Jesus."
>
> - From *The Right One*

she was alone, and she does remember that meeting, because I complimented her on her delicious dessert. I knew that she had a boyfriend, but I figured that all was fair in love and war. Anytime he wasn't around, she was fair game!

Eighteen months later, she had broken up with her boyfriend and the two of us were planning our wedding. I'd never considered myself a smooth operator, but this time I had all the right moves. It was history's most successful coup, and this year we'll be celebrating our twenty-ninth wedding anniversary.

My kids' friends give me "mad respect" for pulling that one off!

It's been a long time since I've been in the dating game, but there are some things in life you never forget. One of those things is what it feels like to be single, and looking for the right marriage partner. It's a stage in life that can bring more angst and confusion and trepidation than just about any other earthly dilemma.

Who does the Lord want me to marry? How will I know when I find them? Should I be actively seeking them, or waiting for God to put them in my path? Do I need to be established first? Will they be godly? Will they be faithful? Will they be a good parent to our children? What if I'm too old to have children by then?

How will I know the right one from the wrong one?

At times the fear and uncertainty can feel so overwhelming that it's a wonder any of us actually make it to the altar.

For Christians, the quest for a marriage partner takes on an even greater level of concern, because Christians know how God feels about divorce. In the Christian paradigm, marriage is a lifelong covenantal relationship, and should never be entered into lightly. God really does want us to get it right the first time.

Wherever you are in your journey toward marriage, we're glad you chose to join us in this study. Over the coming weeks, we'll tackle many of the questions you have about finding and marrying the right partner. If you are single and unattached, this is a great opportunity for you to learn all you can about seeking a potential mate. If you are in a dating relationship, you'll learn some important principles about dating with intention, purity, and purpose. If you are engaged to be married, you'll find useful tools for assessing the strength of your relationship. If it isn't healthy and centered on godly principles and ideals, you need to know that now, while you still have time to change your course.

Marriage is a blessing from God, and God loves blessing his children with the best he has to offer. If marriage is in your future, God is ready to help you find the partner you most need.

So stay with us, and thanks for letting us walk with you on this exciting journey!

Jimmy and Frank

Session One

Searching for a "Soul Mate"

*"Success in marriage does not come merely
through finding the right mate, but through being the right mate."*
- Barnett Brickner

The Right Approach

Why Kendra is still single is a mystery to me. She's bright, pretty, stylish, socially engaging, and tons of fun to be around. She's a Spirit-filled believer, and fully in love with Jesus. She spends much of her time in a large community of believers, with many eligible Christian men her age. And she has been praying for years that God would bring the right man into her life. This year she turned thirty, yet she still sees no real prospects on the horizon.

So why is Kendra still single? It's a question everyone in her circle of friends seems to be asking.

Are all the single men in her life blind? Don't they see what a prize she is? How does a young woman so right for marriage always end up being the bridesmaid and never the bride? Is she doing something to push men away? Is she secretly afraid of commitment? Is she just being too picky?

Kendra knows that people wonder why she isn't married, but she's learned to take it in stride. In fact, Kendra seems to be the only one who isn't worried about her future. Because in spite of the pressure she feels from her friends and family, in spite of the many years she has waited, in spite of the way it might look to others, Kendra is intent on waiting for God to bring *The Right One* into her life.

She also knows how dangerous it would be to panic and settle for the wrong one.

A Spirit of Faith

Kendra would like to find the right partner, but she's not obsessed with the idea. She would like to get married and have children, but she also trusts in God's timing. She looks for opportunities to meet Christian men her age, and even keeps her eyes open for guys that might catch her attention, but she's committed to leaving her future in God's hands. And that's exactly what she should be doing—along with every other young person in her situation.

> "Most people might believe that being "soul mates" is the key to building a happy marriage, but the fact is, good communication is what makes the difference. It is through healthy and effective communication that couples learn how to become soul mates."
>
> - From *The Right One*

Single people who long to be married have two choices. They can search for a potential mate in a spirit of *fear*, or a spirit of *faith*.

A spirit of *fear* says, *What if the right one comes along and I miss them? What if I can't get anyone to notice me? If I don't find the right person now, all of the good ones will be taken!*

But a spirit of *faith* says, *I know that God has my best interest in mind. I know that his timing is perfect. I know that he will make it happen when the time is right.*

Fear doesn't believe that God is big enough, or good enough, or loving enough to take care of our every need. But *faith* trusts implicitly that God is in control, even when it seems that he isn't.

The "Soul Mate" Myth

So does God have a specific "soul mate" in mind for you? Does he have one in mind for Kendra? Or as Christians, should we even use the phrase "soul mate?" Isn't that a secular concept?

The truth is, God does want to see you in a lifelong relationship with your *soul mate,* but you won't find them glancing at you from across a crowded room. A "soul mate" is not someone you find; it's something you create. When you build a life with the right person, you become *soul mates.*

Scripture calls it becoming "one flesh," but it's basically the same thing. When you commit your life in marriage, God binds your hearts together in a supernatural way. You become one in heart, mind, and body. You literally *become one* in the eyes of God, and *soul mate* is good way to describe the process.

Today, Karen and I (Jimmy) are card-carrying *soul mates,* in every sense of the word. We are as connected as any two people could possibly become. But it wasn't that way when we first got married. It was something that God did in,

> "Waiting is part of the process of becoming what God wants us to be."
>
> – John Ortberg

through, and with our relationship after years of serving each other's needs and desires.

So is the "soul mate myth" a myth? I'd say no. But it is an entirely misunderstood concept in many circles. If you're looking for your *soul mate,* you're likely to be sorely disappointed. Look instead for someone who shares your values and vision for the future, someone who loves God as much as you do, someone who meets the criteria you have for a life partner, someone that God has clearly brought into your life for a reason, and then allow God to lead you on your journey toward becoming one.

The Right Reading

Read Proverbs 18:22; Proverbs 19:14; Philippians 4:19

The Right Questions

In what ways can you relate to Kendra's situation? Have you been praying for the right person to come along, only to find yourself still waiting? Or is your situation different?

If you've been looking and praying for a marriage partner, why do you think God hasn't brought them to you yet?

Have you ever been in a serious dating relationship? If so, what were some positive and negative aspects of your relationship?

Have you ever felt panicked that you may never find the right person? Describe what caused you to feel that way, and how you moved past it.

Why is it so hard to move forward in *faith*, instead of *fear* when it comes to waiting for the right marriage partner?

What are three specific things you can do to help maintain a perspective of *faith* while waiting for the right person?
1.
2.
3.

What comes to mind when you hear the term "soul mate?"

What do you think it takes for married couples to become *soul mates* (as defined by today's reading)?

List three married couples you know that you would consider *soul mates*.

1.

2.

3.

What traits or habits do you see in these couples that you hope to have someday in your own marriage?

Do you think it's wrong to actively search for the right marriage partner? Or should we simply wait on the Lord and pray? Explain why.

> "The folly of not waiting for God is that we forfeit the blessing of having God work for us."
>
> – John Piper

How would you describe a healthy and godly approach to looking for a future spouse?

The Right Discussion

1) As a group, discuss why it is so hard to wait on God when searching for the right marriage partner. Do we lack faith? Are we being impatient? Are we taking the wrong approach?

2) Re-read Proverbs 18:22 and discuss what God is saying to us through this passage.

3) Re-read Proverbs 19:14. Why do you think the Proverbs writer is so specific in writing that wives are "from the Lord?" What are the implications of this truth? Are not houses and land also from the Lord? Is it safe to say that husbands are from the Lord as well?

4) Ask if anyone is willing to discuss their own personal journey of looking for the right mate.

5) Discuss some specific things you hope to learn or experience through the course of this study.

6) Re-read Philippians 4:19. Talk about what God is saying to singles in this passage. How does this thought bring you comfort? How should it affect our attitude and actions knowing that God always has our best interest in mind?

The Right Response

End today's discussion in a time of prayer and reflection. Pray that God would give you peace of mind and a right perspective as you wait on his perfect timing. If any thoughts or ideas from today's lesson brought conviction or repentance to your spirit, note those things in the space below. Commit this week to praying specifically about these things.

_____

_____

_____

_____

_____

_____

_____

_____

Session Two

Exposing the
Myths of Love

"Sacrificial love has transforming power... The person who truly loves does so because of a decision to love. This person has made a commitment to be loving whether or not the loving feeling is present."
- Dr. M. Scott Peck

The Right Approach

My wife and daughter have watched *Pride and Prejudice* more times than they can remember. We own both versions—the 2-hour feature film, and the 6-hour TV miniseries. They've watched them both so many times that they can quote most of the lines by heart. And they often do during dinner conversations, or when cooking together in the kitchen. They even have the British accents down pat.

If you were to ask them what they most love about the story, they would likely talk about the elegant colonial wardrobe of the day, or the graceful way that women carried themselves, or the beautiful way that people spoke. Jane Austen fills her books with words like "auspicate," and "incandescently," and "fulsome." Words that I'm certain I've never once used in a book until this moment.

> "When we see love as a feeling, it will always fail us, because feelings are fickle. They change with the tides. They can't be trusted. Feelings are unstable and fleeting, and almost always biased. Emotions can't be trusted."
>
> - From *The Right One*

I know, though, that what they really love about the story is Mr. Darcy, the tall, handsome, wealthy, charming, and mysteriously soft-spoken lead character. Mr. Darcy is the bane of every other guy's existence. He's practically perfect, always calm and collected, always coming to the rescue, always walking upright with his hands folded behind his back. Girls swoon whenever he walks into a room, though he's much too humble to notice.

Yeah, makes me sick too.

Mr. Darcy is the proverbial knight in shining armor. The kinsman redeemer who rescues the fair maiden Elizabeth from poverty and humiliation, and sweeps her away to his mansion, where the two of them marry and live happily ever after. It's a love story that grips the hardest heart, and is as timeless as it is moving. It isn't hard to see why the women in my house are so enamored by the story. They know it's just a fairy tale, but like just about every other woman on the planet, my wife and daughter are unashamedly in love with love.

The truth is, I enjoy the story myself, though I'm not as quick to admit it. Because down deep we are all just a little in love with love. Even those of us who get giddy over a "Jason Bourne" marathon.

When Love is a Feeling

There's plenty of room in life for a little fantasy, so I'm not out to demonize the "Jane Austen book club." The world is filled with fairy tales because stories of love and romance fill a deep need within all of our hearts. We all long to be loved, and we want that love to be profound and long lasting. We are hard-wired to desire a meaningful connection with someone who fills our hearts with passion. We want to love, and to be loved, because that's how God created us.

The trouble comes when we take a storybook fantasy paradigm with us into the real life world of romantic relationships. When we begin seeing love as a feeling. As an emotion that overcomes us as we see Mr. or Ms. Right glancing in our direction across a crowded room. As a sense of euphoria that comes into our spirit whenever our "one true love" is near.

This all may sound over-exaggerated, but trust me, I've known grown men and women who wanted so much for their romantic fantasies to be real that they sacrificed all hint of dignity and common sense to make it happen. And not one of them ever found what they were looking for.

The problem with seeing love as a feeling is that it takes effort and responsibility out of the equation. We no longer have to look for love; we just wait for it to find us. We're no longer accountable for making a relationship work, because the decision is made *for* us, not *by* us. If love brought us together, love will keep us together. And if the feelings don't last, it just wasn't meant to be.

It certainly makes the dating process much easier.

> "I'm convinced that almost all failed marriages began as dysfunctional dating relationships—even those that lasted twenty or thirty years before coming to an end."
>
> - From *The Right One*

The truth is, love is not a feeling or an emotion, and most of us know that. At least on an intellectual level. We all claim to know the difference between truth and fiction. But do we know it on even a subconscious level? Do we understand that fact in the core of our spirits, where it matters most? Or have we been subtly and subliminally conditioned to believe otherwise?

The Search for Love

I'm convinced that the primary cause of most failed marriages is unrealistic expectations. And expectations are almost always rooted in fantasies. In our hearts, we expect love to look and feel like it does on the big screen, and when it doesn't, we wonder why. Hollywood has portrayed love as an emotion for so long, and so often, that most of us find it impossible to truly separate fantasy from reality.

It's no secret that the divorce rate is much too high, but with all the mixed messages, I'm actually surprised it isn't higher.

So how should all of this change your approach to dating? If you want to be successful, it should change everything.

If you've found yourself waiting and watching for your "one true love," then that's a search you need to abandon. Because that person doesn't exist. If you've been seeking someone to fill a "Mr. Darcy-shaped" hole in your heart, then it's time to put away the romance novels and get realistic. Mr. Darcy is about as real as your faulty expectations—and would likely let you down just as fast, even if you did find him. If you've been leading with your hormones instead of your head, waiting for a woman who cooks like your mother, looks like Megan Fox, and worships the ground you walk on, you may need to lower your expectations a bit. Or at least buy a mirror.

If you've been searching for a storybook romance, some once-in-a-lifetime connection with a "soul mate" created just for you, it might be time to rethink your view and understanding of *true love*.

I've never seen a 12-step program for that kind of thing, but do have a thought to get you started.

Retrain Your Heart

A healthy approach to dating happens when you begin to retrain your heart and mind to see love as an action verb. Not as a feeling, but as a determined act of the will. It's not something you experience; it's something you choose to do. It's not an emotion; it's an ability. It's not something that happens to you; it's something you nurture and orchestrate and develop.

> "The world takes us to a silver screen on which flickering images of passion and romance play, and as we watch, the world says, "This is love." God takes us to the foot of a tree on which a naked and bloodied man hangs and says, "This is love."
>
> – Joshua Harris

Love is a deliberate and determined act of the will. There is nothing idle or passive about it. It doesn't wane or fail when life gets tough; it only grows stronger and more resolved. It's the bond that keeps your relationship from drifting when every storm in the ocean is raging to tear you apart. It's the one thing you can depend on when all of life seems bent on pulling you down.

Love is what happens when two emotionally healthy people come together and decide to join their lives in marriage, and then do whatever it takes to build a life-long, non-negotiable, covenantal relationship with each other.

When searching for a life partner, don't trust the decision to feelings or emotion. Instead look for someone who is healthy, stable, and realistic. Someone who shares your love for God, who laughs at all your jokes, who loves the way you smile, and who is just as committed as you are to building a meaningful life together.

Don't dumb down your expectations. Maybe just rethink them a bit. Look for qualities that are intrinsic, and eternal, and meaningful for the long haul.

The Right Reading

1 Corinthians 13:4-8, 13; Colossians 3:12-14; 1 John 3:18

The Right Questions

List 3 of your favorite romantic books or movies.

a.

b.

c.

What is it about these stories that most touches your heart?

If you had to summarize the "myths of love" portrayed in these stories, how would you describe them?

Why are these types of myths so damaging to society—in particular young, impressionable people?

What are some specific ways that you think these "love myths" have affected single, dating people today?

Do you see this same dynamic among your community of single friends and acquaintances? If so, why do you think that's true?

In your own words, what happens when we start seeing love as a feeling?

In what way(s) does seeing love as a feeling take effort and responsibility out of the equation?

How does it affect a dating relationship when single people base their actions more on fantasy than reality?

Have you ever been guilty of that? Explain why or why not.

Have you ever been rejected by someone who once had feelings for you but lost interest? Would you be willing to share your story with the group?

Have you ever had feelings for someone else and then lost interest? What do you think caused your feelings to change?

What happens in a dating relationship when one or both partners base their love on feelings instead of commitment?

Have you ever known a couple who divorced because they "fell out of love?" How did their break-up affect those around them?

What advice would you give to couples who might be struggling to stay connected with each other?

The Right Discussion

1) If it's true that the cause of most failed marriages is unrealistic expectations, discuss where these expectations come from.

2) Do you feel that some of your expectations for a dating partner are unrealistic? If so, how can you go about retraining your heart and mind to think differently?

3) Read 1 Corinthians 13:4-8. Paul describes the many characteristics of love. In the NIV version, he lists 16 different ways in which sacrificial love is evident in the life of a believer. As you read these character traits aloud, discuss why each one is critical to a healthy and happy marriage. And what happens when they are not present. For example, "Why is it important for couples to be patient with each other?" "What happens in a marriage when couples have a habit of being impatient?" And so on.

4) Discuss what all of these character traits have in common.

5) Read 1 Corinthians 13:13. In what way is love different than "faith" and "hope?" What makes love greater than faith and hope?

6) Read Colossians 3:12-14. Discuss how this passage might apply to people who are preparing their hearts for a future marriage relationship. And what does Paul mean when he says that love binds all these virtues together in "perfect unity?"

7) Read 1 John 3:18. Discuss some specific ways that couples can apply this passage as they navigate a dating relationship.

8) We've established the fact that in marriage, seeing love as a decision is critical to the health and strength of the relationship. But why is it so important that dating people train their hearts to understand and internalize this truth now, while they are still looking for a marriage partner?

9) Discuss some specific ways that single people can train their hearts to start seeing marriage as a decision of the will instead of a feeling.

The Right Response

As you end this session in prayer, ask God to help you start seeing love the way that he would have you define it. Pray specifically for those things you need to do in order to learn sacrificial love as you prepare your hearts and lives for a future marriage. Write out the most critical lessons you learned in today's session, and commit to praying about those things over the coming week.

_____

_____

Session Three

Healthy and Realistic Expectations

"We've seen many singles who are so tired of waiting for their ship to come in that they don't even have the energy to go to the proverbial dock. Sometimes it's because their expectations are sky high."
- Dr. Les Parrott

The Right Approach

During high school and college, I (Frank) worked in a bakery, and my boss was a man we all called Sandy. He was actually more of a mentor to me than a boss.

One day I was lamenting over a girl I knew at school that I was somewhat interested in. She was bright and funny and a very committed Christian. She had almost all of the qualities I was attracted to in a girl, except she wasn't a raving beauty. She was very cute, just not the "Barbie with a Bible degree" I was hoping to find.

Sandy listened to me whine, then turned to me and asked, "So, how many beauty contests have you won this year?"

I think I got his point.

There's something about being single that tends to skew a person's view of reality. Maybe it's because there are so few people in our lives willing to bring us down a notch when we start to get haughty. From the time we're old enough to listen, we hear our parents tell us how cute and wonderful and exceptional we are, so we start to believe it. But what most of us need in life is someone willing to be honest.

The truth is, you are not perfect, and the person you marry won't be perfect, either. And that's not a bad thing. Our flaws are what make us unique, and keep us humble. God uses our flaws to grow us into what he wants us to become, and we never really stop becoming.

> "Realistic expectations are not about hope without honesty, and they are not about honesty without hope. Realism is found at the intersection of unabashed honesty and uncompromising hope."
>
> – Paul David Tripp

If you're looking for a really great marriage partner, look for someone who knows their flaws and shortcomings and is willing to grow. Someone who readily admits that they have issues, and is ready to mature and work through them in order to build a healthy, lifelong relationship.

When I (Jimmy) married Karen, I had many terrible flaws. I think my flaws even had flaws. I didn't know that at the time, but it wasn't long before God exposed them and convicted me to change. I loved Karen deeply, and wanted our marriage to work, so I set out on a journey toward becoming a better husband. God began to change me from the inside out. I was a million miles from perfect, but what I had was a willingness to change and grow in order to become the husband that Karen needed.

Today we have an incredible marriage. I'm still not perfect—I never will be this side of heaven—but I continue to work through my shortcomings as God exposes them. Karen does the same for me. Our goal in marriage is always to be the person the other most needs, and that has been one of the primary keys to our lifelong love affair.

Healthy Expectations

Having said all that, it's still important to have healthy standards when looking for a potential marriage partner. There are many expectations that are very realistic and essential, and you shouldn't be willing to compromise on those things. The key is to learn what you really do want and need from a partner, and then concentrate your search on people who seem to possess those qualities.

There's no one formula for doing that, but here are a few ideas to help you get started.

Get Rid of Your "List"

We all have an unwritten "list" of qualities that we're looking for in a mate, whether spoken or unspoken, and some of them are quite honestly not that important. My (Frank's) daughter Kandilyn has always had a thing for guys with beards, which is a mystery to me, since the men in our family can barely grow facial hair. I'm convinced we're part dolphin. But somehow she's always been attracted to the "Duck Dynasty" look. She's engaged to be married this fall to an awesome young man named Bryson who is very nearly as hairless as I am. She says she almost didn't go out with him because he didn't have a beard, and now she finds it stunning that this was actually on her list of requirements.

> "Happy marriages begin with healthy and realistic expectations. And the best time to discuss those expectations is before heading to the altar."
> - From *The Right One*

The first step in setting realistic expectations is to throw away your list of superficial and unimportant desires and instead focus on things that are truly important.

Understand Your Non-Negotiables

Throwing away your list doesn't mean you've given up on your expectations. We all have non-negotiable standards that should never be compromised. You are better off staying single than to settle for a person who is emotionally abusive, unable to make a living, or is simply unattractive to you. Your goal is to refine your expectations, so that they are healthy and realistic, not non-existent.

As a Christian, the most important quality on your list of non-negotiables should be someone who is just as dedicated to their faith as you are. Someone who loves Jesus, and displays the fruits and qualities that committed believers are supposed to have. Getting into a relationship with someone who doesn't share your faith is a monumental mistake, no matter how you try to justify it. So finding a strong and faithful Christian should be at the top of your list of expectations.

Other things may be important to you as well. If you are extremely athletic and health-conscious, it would be a mistake for you to marry a couch potato. If you grew up on a ranch and dream of owning horses, you wouldn't be happy with a city boy who doesn't know a cow from a chicken and owns a closet full of skinny jeans.

Your non-negotiables are unique to you, and not the same as everyone else's, but they are just as important and valid. So don't be afraid to make that mental list, and then keep it in the forefront of your mind.

Hold Yourself to the Same Standards

Once you've nailed down a clear list of non-negotiable traits you need in a mate, it's time to turn the tables and look in the mirror. Ask yourself if you display the same qualities and character traits that you're expecting from someone else. More than that, do you possess qualities that will actually attract someone who meets those criteria?

> "Do not equate human worth with flawless beauty or handsomeness! If you require physical perfection in your mate, he or she may make the same demands of you. Neither of you will keep it for long. Don't let love escape you because of the false values of your culture."
>
> – Dr. James Dobson

For example, if one of your non-negotiable character traits is a strong and independent person, you won't find them if you are helpless and needy. Not if they are emotionally healthy. If you want someone who is caring and compassionate, those kinds of people will never be attracted to a diva. So make sure you exude the qualities that someone of that caliber is looking for.

If you want to find the right kind of person, begin by being the right kind of person.

Be Flexible and Open Minded

The reality is, the person you think you need may not be the person you find. Because none of us are completely dialed in to what is best for us. God may have a completely different person in mind for you than you have in mind for yourself.

My (Frank's) wife Ruthie was always certain she would marry a preacher or a missionary. It was firmly at the top of her list of non-negotiables during her years in college. When we met, she was dating a Bible major who was preparing to go into the mission field. He had the qualities she was looking for, but God knew that he was completely wrong for her.

When I came along, she never gave me a second look, because I was firmly entrenched in the world of business. She knew what she wanted, and I wasn't it. But God stepped in and changed her plans, and her heart began to change along with them.

At the end of the day, none of us really know what God has planned for our future. So when looking for a potential mate, expect the best, but always give God room to work.

When you're moving in God's will, sometimes the best plan you can make is to plan to be surprised.

The Right Reading

Read 2 Corinthians 6:14; Psalm 37:4; Psalm 84:11; Romans 8:28

The Right Questions

How would you rate your expectations for a potential marriage partner? Are you realistic? Somewhat realistic? Entirely unrealistic?

Where do you think your expectations come from?

Often we believe our expectations come from our own needs and desires, when they are really handed down to us from our parents, grandparents, or even a mentor. Can you see the influence of others when you look at your unspoken list of requirements? Elaborate on your answer.

Often unrealistic expectations are rooted in our own wounds and insecurities. Someone who has struggled with their weight in the past may be completely unwilling to date anyone who is carrying a few extra pounds. Someone who is self-conscious about their red hair and freckles may push away anyone with similar features. Do you see this in yourself in any way? Explain.

List 5 unspoken expectations you've had that you now believe might be unrealistic.
1.
2.
3.
4.
5.

Now list 5 unspoken expectations that you believe are realistic. Maybe not deal-breakers, but at least healthy desires.
1.
2.
3.
4.
5.

Take time to discuss these 5 expectations, and why you think they are important.

There is a difference between "expectations" and "requirements." Requirements are those things that you consider non-negotiable—like a strong faith in God. Below, list what you consider to be the top 8 non-negotiable requirements you need to find in a future mate.

1.

2.

3.

4.

5.

6.

7.

8.

Next, beside each of these 8 non-negotiables, rate them on a scale of 1 to 5 in importance (1 being the most important). Discuss your reason behind these ratings with the group.

Look over your list of non-negotiables. Which 3 of these traits or characteristics do you believe you possess to a strong degree?

List 3 of these traits or characteristics you wish you possessed to a greater degree, but are aware that you probably need to work on.

In a few sentences, describe the person you would consider your "dream mate." And be specific. How would they look? What would they do? What kind of character and personality would they have? How would they act? Be creative, and list any characteristic you can think of.

Now look back at your answer and be completely honest: did you just describe yourself? The opposite of yourself? Someone you know?

Discuss why you think you answered this way. Is God trying to tell you something about your expectations for a mate?

The Right Discussion

1) Re-read 2 Corinthians 6:14, and discuss why Paul warns Christians so sternly against marrying people outside the faith. What would you say to someone who fell for an unbeliever and thinks that they can turn their heart toward Christ once they are married? Why is "missionary dating" such a bad idea?

2) Chances are good that someone in your group will have a story or example that seems to run counter to Paul's warning—maybe someone they knew who married an unbeliever, and then later brought them to Christ. Does this validate the concept of "missionary dating?"

3) Re-read Psalm 37:4. What does this passage have to say to singles who are worried that they'll never find the right person?

4) If God has promised to give us the "desires of our heart," then why should any of our expectations for marriage be considered unrealistic? Shouldn't he give us even the smallest wish when it comes to a life partner? If not, why not?

5) Read Psalm 84:11. What does it take on our end to expect "good things" from God? Discuss why God would put stipulations on us before bestowing his favor on our lives. If we are saved by grace alone, then why would works be expected before receiving God's blessing?

6) Re-read Romans 8:28. How should we apply this promise from God when it comes to looking for the right marriage partner?

7) In what ways should this promise bring comfort to you during your single stage of life?

8) Read 1 Corinthians 7:7-8 and discuss Paul's meaning. Is he saying that some people have the gift of singleness? If so, what does that mean?

9) In Genesis 2:18, God said it is not good for man to be alone. If that is true, why would he expect some people to remain single?

10) Most single people assume that they will someday be married, but it appears that God does call a small percentage of people to remain single. How would you feel if you discovered that this is God's plan for your future? Would it frustrate you? Shake your faith? Would you accept it? Would you welcome it?

The Right Response

As you end in prayer, take a few minutes to re-read your list of non-negotiable requirements for a marriage partner. Ask God to speak to you regarding these expectations. If you sense that any of these requirements are unrealistic or selfish, make a note of that in the space below, and commit to praying about it during the coming week.

Also, pray specifically that God would open your heart and mind to whatever he has in store for your future, and pledge to follow, wherever he might lead.

_____

_____

_____

_____

_____

_____

_____

_____

_____

_____

_____

_____

Session Four

The Right (and Wrong) Way to Date

"God is more interested in your future and your relationships than you are."
- Billy Graham

The Right Approach

I recently heard someone say that there are only two possible outcomes for a dating relationship. Either you break up, or you get married. Maybe that's why single people seem to be so tied up in knots over the process.

I (Frank) honestly don't remember that being the mindset when I was single and dating. If I was attracted to a girl, and thought she wouldn't say no, I would ask her out. The date was usually dinner and a movie, and if there were no sparks, it would be our last date. This led to a lot of last dates, but I don't think there were many hurt feelings over it. My dates got free food, and I got a little more experience in how to act in the company of a lady. No harm, no foul.

Today, though, young people seem to take dating much more seriously, especially in

Christian circles. I think it's because our culture has become hyper sensitive to self-esteem issues, and we're all afraid of hurting someone else's feelings.

Whatever the cause, today's Christian singles spend a lot of time "hanging out" in coffee shops and almost no time going out on actual dates. And it frustrates Christian women to no end. I hear them regularly lament that men have no idea what to do when it comes to courting a young woman. They are far too passive and unwilling to let a girl know that they might be interested.

Somewhere between serial dating and never dating is a healthy balance, and maybe that's what we should be striving for.

Date to Gauge Interest

Men have their side of the story too, and they say it is usually women who take dating too seriously. Often a man will ask a girl out to simply gauge interest, but by the end of the first date she's already picking out shower curtains. There's a difference between gauging interest and determining compatibility. It takes a little time to decide if you are really interested in pursuing a relationship with someone, and when they jump ahead of the game, it makes every conversation awkward.

> "The Bible gives a wealth of instruction and advice on what healthy relationships look like, and the importance of sexual and moral purity. And couples who ignore these warnings in their dating relationships are bound to suffer."
> -From *The Right One*

Our son David is twenty-five and still single, and he seldom dates, but he does spend a lot of time hanging out at coffee shops with friends. If he meets a girl he might be interested in pursuing, that's usually the first place they go. In his mind, "hanging out" over coffee is the new dinner and a movie paradigm. It's how single people get to know each other in order to assess their level of interest.

The trouble I see with this approach is that it's easy for guys to string girls along. And girls can't tell if a guy is pursuing a relationship, or just enjoys her as a friend. The lines are very blurred. And that is what frustrates single women the most. There is no verbal intent of interest, and often there isn't even an implied one, so they are left wondering where they stand.

To David's credit, he doesn't believe in playing with a girl's heart, so he's quick to clear up any mixed signals someone may be getting. If he is interested in pursuing a relationship with a girl, he has an intentional conversation to let her know that. If he's not, but feels that she might be wondering, he'll usually let her know that as well. He has yet to find the right girl, but when he does, she won't be left wondering what he is thinking, because he's always open and honest about his intentions.

> "There is a godly way to date, and that is what you want your relationship to look like if you are seeking God's guidance and direction."
> -From *The Right One*

I actually think this is a very healthy approach to dating. If single men were more direct and communicative regarding their intentions, single women wouldn't feel as frustrated and confused. It would become a much more open and deliberate process.

Date With Honor and Purity

Another reason today's dating scene has become so awkward and unsure is that lines of physical and mental purity have become so blurred. This is true even among Christians.

In a recent survey conducted by ChristianMingle.com, Christian singles between the ages of 18 to 59 were asked, "Would you have sex before marriage?" Sixty-three percent of respondents answered "yes."

Oddly enough, in the same survey, Christian singles were asked how important "praying and going to church" was when looking for a future spouse, and the vast majority answered "highly desirable."[1]

There was a time when everyone understood that sex before marriage was wrong and sinful, but that doesn't appear to be the case anymore. And it's a very sad and dangerous paradigm shift.

In God's economy, sexual promiscuity is clearly unacceptable. It isn't just a bad idea; it is sin in the highest form—and yes, some sins are worse than others. Paul tells us in 1 Corinthians 6:18, "Every other sin a person commits is outside the body, but the sexually immoral person sins against his own body."

Sexual sins are worse than others because they do so much more damage. They affect us spiritually, mentally, emotionally, physically, and relationally. They not only harm us, but those around us, and even our future relationships.

Within the context of marriage, sex is a wonderful and sacred thing. It is the most intimate and spiritually bonding experience that a couple can have. But sex outside of marriage is detached and disruptive and disrespectful. It is never right, and should never be part of a healthy and honoring dating relationship.

Date With Intention

Ultimately, dating is a means to an end. The purpose of dating is to eventually find someone you'd like to spend the rest of your life with, and someone who would like to spend the rest of their life with you. Most couples don't find each other by accident; they have to actively work at it. And to do it right takes a high level of intentionality.

> "When God knows you're ready for the responsibility of commitment, He'll reveal the right person under the right circumstances."
>
> – Joshua Harris

The healthiest relationships—and the ones most prepared for marriage—are those that take a very purposeful and deliberate approach to the dating process. Once two people have determined that they like each other enough to begin pursuing a possible marriage relationship, their dating process takes on a much greater level of focus and intent.

When you get to that point, it's time to take a more measured approach. And here are a few ways to do that:

Articulate Your Feelings

Talk about your desire to take your relationship to the next level, and what that means in the context of dating. What will your dating relationship look like going forward? Are you both prepared to commit to the relationship and to date each other exclusively? Are you both willing to be completely open and honest about your feelings? And do you commit to honoring each other as you set out to assess your compatibility for marriage?

Commit to Honoring God

There is a marked difference between a Christian dating relationship and a secular one, and that difference should be easily apparent to others. When Christians date, everything they say or do as a couple should be honoring to God, first and foremost. This means spending time in prayer, asking God for both confirmation and blessing as you set out to get to know each other better.

Set Clear and Healthy Boundaries

There's more to staying pure than simply not having sex. A truly pure dating relationship means maintaining purity of heart, mind, and body. And the best way to do that is to set very clear and healthy boundaries—both physically and emotionally. This may mean deciding not to spend time alone in each other's rooms or apartments, and not allowing yourself to cross some well-defined boundaries of physical affection. Healthy and honorable dating means being willing to do whatever it takes to keep yourself pure—sexually and emotionally.

> "Sexual familiarity can be deadly to a relationship. In addition to the many moral, spiritual, and physical reasons for remaining virgins until marriage, there are numerous psychological and interpersonal advantages as well."
>
> – Dr. James Dobson

Have Intentional Conversations

What are your hopes and dreams for the future? Where do you hope to be five, ten, or twenty years from now? What kind of family do you hope to have? Where do you hope to live? What is most important to you in life?

These are the kinds of conversations that help couples gauge their level of compatibility, and decide if they are going the same direction in life. Your goal is to learn all you can about each other's true inner thoughts and character—to discover if you are equally yoked and compatible, if you share the same spiritual values and beliefs. You're trying to determine if this is the person you are willing to commit to for the rest of your life. And it takes intentional conversations to know those things.

Trust God

Ultimately, every decision that we make in life should be placed at God's feet, especially such a life-changing one. And any relationship we enter into should be immersed in prayer. Pray consistently about every aspect of your relationship, and then trust God to reveal his will for your future. Believe that God wants what is best for your future, and that he will make it clear to you if the one you are dating is the right one for you.

The Right Reading

Read 1 Thessalonians 4:3-7; 1 Corinthians 6:18-20; Psalm 119:30

The Right Questions

Do you agree that dating today among Christian singles has become more awkward and non-committal? If so, how?

Why do you think men today are less inclined to ask single women out?

Do you agree that single women tend to get ahead of themselves in dating? If so, how?

How would you describe a healthy approach to singles getting to know each other in order to determine their level of interest?

It has been documented that Christian singles today are far more likely to engage in sex before marriage. Have you found that to be true among your circle of friends? Explain.
Why do you think this is true? What has changed in the culture over the last few years to add to this problem?

Read Psalm 119:30. What does this passage say to you personally about maintaining sexual and mental purity while dating?

How would you describe a healthy and intentional dating process?

In what way(s) have your dating relationships in the past not been healthy?

In what way(s) have they not been intentional?

In what ways should a Christian dating relationship look different than a secular one? Be specific.

What are some examples of clear and healthy boundaries that couples can set in order to maintain purity of heart and body?

What are some examples of intentional conversations that a couple should have in order to assess their level of compatibility?

When you pray about your relationships (and your future relationships), how do you pray?

Summarize today's lesson in one succinct sentence.

The Right Discussion

1) Re-read 1 Thessalonians 4:3-7. Discuss why sexual immorality is such an affront to God's holiness and character.

2) In this passage, why does God equate sexual immorality with taking advantage of a brother or sister? If pre-marital sex is just sex between "consenting adults" why does God see it as taking advantage?

3) Re-read 1 Corinthians 6:18-20. What should be our response when sexual temptation comes our way? What are some concrete ways to obey this command?

4) Why is sex outside of marriage dishonoring to God? And why is it never acceptable in God's eyes?

5) Read Hebrews 13:4. Discuss what it looks like to have a God-honoring relationship in the context of marriage.

6) What does it look like to have a God-honoring dating relationship before marriage?

The Right Response

In the space below, make a note of any point or principle from today's lesson that spoke to your heart. Is there anything about your dating habits you feel convicted to change? Is there anything you plan to do differently in your future relationships? Commit to praying about these things this week during your times of prayer.

_____

_____

Session Five

Recognizing Red Flags

"Life is too short to sacrifice yourself for someone who will never appreciate you and is incapable of loving you."
- Lisa Scott

The Right Approach

I think the only thing worse than being a narcissist is trying to maintain a relationship with one. It can be a monumental exercise in futility.

Several years ago, I (Frank) got into a short-term business arrangement with a friend who I soon discovered was a textbook narcissist. He had perhaps the first full-blown case of Narcissistic Personality Disorder I had ever run across, and trying to navigate a business relationship with him was wholly impossible. He was incapable of listening to others when it came to making decisions, and would rather see the project fail than to admit that he might be wrong. He took credit for every success and blamed anyone he could when things didn't go as planned.

When the project was over, he and I parted ways and the friendship imploded altogether.

I've never been so happy to be free of dealing with someone on a daily basis. In hindsight, I blame myself for agreeing to work with him on the project. There were many red flag warnings at the outset that I should have heeded.

> "Too many Christian women today have ended up with an Ishmael because impatience pushed them into an unhappy marriage. Please take my fatherly advice: You are much better off single than with the wrong guy!"
>
> – J. Lee Grady

Thankfully, our business arrangement wasn't a long-term one. I can't imagine being married to someone so egocentric and unreasonable. But it happens all the time, simply because people choose to ignore red flag warnings during the dating phase of the relationship.

Red flag warnings are easy to spot, and important to watch for when assessing the strength—or weakness—of a dating relationship. And these red flags rarely get better as time goes on. They are there to keep you out of trouble, and if you are praying about your relationship, God will clearly reveal them to you before it is too late. You just have to commit to keeping your eyes wide open, and your heart ready to listen.

Here are a few of the more prominent red flags you should be watching for while seeking a healthy dating relationship. Ignoring any of these red flags can lead to trouble in the future.

Control Issues

Issues of control and domination may be the most common problem I (Jimmy) see during premarital counseling. Control issues can vary in degree, from simply wanting to be in charge of the relationship, to a need to control every aspect of a partner's life, like what they wear, what they say, who they talk to, where they go, and what they are doing every minute of the day. Severe issues of dominance are easy to spot, and extremely dangerous for the weaker partner. But more common are those subtle issues of control that are harder to expose. One partner may be strong-willed while the other is somewhat passive, making the relationship one-sided. The passive partner simply allows the other to make most of the decisions without complaining.

This type of co-dependent relationship often works during the dating phase, but in marriage, it can create an enormous amount of conflict and struggle.

Physical or Verbal Abuse

Not all controlling relationships become outwardly abusive, but when they do, it can quickly turn into a dangerous and volatile situation. Abuse, in any form, can never be overlooked or taken lightly, and it always gets worse.

The most common form of abuse in dating relationships is verbal. And it tends to begin rather subtly. One partner begins joking about the other, or putting them down, and these verbal attacks slowly escalate. It's almost as if they are gauging how much verbal abuse the other is willing to take without leaving. Little by little, the attacks get more personal and vicious. Soon they find themselves in a full-blown verbally abusive relationship. And verbal abuse can easily lead to physical abuse.

This is a non-negotiable deal-breaker in any relationship, and should never be tolerated—even in small doses.

Anger Issues

The biggest problem with anger issues is that they are easy to hide from friends and family, and dating partners have a tendency to keep it hidden from others. It's an embarrassing issue to deal with, both for the victim and the offender. Since we all get angry from time to time, saying someone has a "problem" with anger is a subjective judgment. And no one wants to be judgmental.

> "Strong marriages begin as healthy dating relationships. And the healthier you date, the greater chance you have for a long and happy marriage."
> - From *The Right One*

But anger issues are a big deal in the context of marriage, and they need to be identified and dealt with before standing at the altar. Otherwise, you could be setting yourself up for a lot of pain and conflict.

Dishonesty

When couples catch each other lying, or harboring secrets, it puts an enormous strain on the relationship. Trust is an imperative ingredient to marriage. It is the foundation of safety and security that you have to have in order for the marriage to stand. Without it, you have almost no hope of building a strong and healthy marriage.

If you can't trust your partner to be honest with you while dating, don't kid yourself into thinking that it will somehow change after you're married. It will only get worse.

A Pattern of Conflict

It's always a curious thing when couples who can't seem to get along decide that they want to get married. As if they are somehow eager to take their fighting to the next level. But I (Jimmy) see it all the time when engaged couples come to me for counseling. And too often, they don't seem to be able to recognize this as a problem.

When couples have a pattern of conflict, it's usually a sign that they are incompatible, and the best approach is for them to go their separate ways now, before it is too late. Constant bickering is not a typical part of dating. It's a sign that something between you is not working.

Overdependence on Parents

A lack of independence is a growing problem among today's young people, and it's a huge red flag to watch for. If you are dating a young man in his early twenties who is still being supported by his parents, maybe still living at home, it could be a sign of arrested adolescence. Maybe he is lazy, and has trouble holding down a good job. Or perhaps he just doesn't have a strong work ethic. It's a bad idea to assume that he will suddenly grow up once he decides to get married.

And it goes both ways. If you are dating a young woman who is still dependent on her parents, who isn't expected to cook or clean or do the laundry, and who couldn't survive without her parents' help, it might be a red flag warning. Maybe not, but it's something to carefully consider.

> "Beware of blindness to obvious warning signs that tell you that your potential husband or wife is basically disloyal, hateful, spiritually uncommitted, hooked on drugs or alcohol, given to selfishness, etc. Believe me, a bad marriage is far worse than the most lonely instance of singleness."
>
> –Dr. James Dobson

Mood Swings

Unstable emotions can be another dangerous red flag warning. Some people may struggle with a manic-depressive personality, even if they haven't been diagnosed. Or maybe they have grown up in a dysfunctional home and have never had a healthy model of acting and reacting to situations. Or maybe they are simply wired to be over-emotional, and struggle to keep their mood swings in check.

Whatever the cause, it's a sign that something isn't quite right in their personality, and shouldn't be ignored.

An Air of Disrespect

If you sense that your dating partner is treating you with disrespect, that's not a feeling that you should ignore. Maybe they make little jokes at your expense, or tend to tease you with sarcasm. Perhaps they criticize you in front of friends, or use belittling language when they're angry. Or maybe they just blatantly talk disrespectfully to you.

This is not something you can overlook. Sarcasm is not funny; it is textbook passive-aggressive behavior. Below the surface there is always a level of contempt and condescension. Joking and belittling language is far from harmless. It is blatant bullying, and usually grows worse with time.

> "Marriage is one decision in life that God expects you to get right the first time. So don't allow yourself to be rushed. And don't make a mistake you'll regret for the rest of your life."
> - From *The Right One*

Dysfunctional Family

All families deal with a certain level of dysfunction. We are imperfect people, saved by grace, and are expected to extend grace to those around us. If you run across a seemingly perfect family, run as fast as you can, because they're likely hiding bones in the basement.

You can't expect your dating partner's family to be perfect, but you can hope for a certain level of normalcy and function. Highly dysfunctional families have a way of breeding dysfunctional children. It's impossible to get through childhood without being affected by the way your parents act and react. A dysfunctional family is not necessarily a reason to break off a relationship, but it is a red flag to watch for.

Trust Your Instincts

Ultimately, when it comes to recognizing relational red flags, you have to trust your instincts. If you have a general uneasy feeling about your partner or your relationship, that's a feeling you shouldn't ignore, even if you can't quite put your finger on the problem. If everything about your relationship looks good on paper but still leaves you feeling anxious and concerned, it might be the still small voice of the Holy Spirit speaking to your heart.

Then again, it might be cold feet or a bad slice of pizza, but you won't know for sure unless you take time to seek God's guidance and do some reevaluation.

The Right Reading

Proverbs 18:14-15; Proverbs 22:24-25; Proverbs 25:24; Luke 6:43-45

The Right Questions

Have you ever been in a relationship with someone who showed unhealthy personality issues, like narcissism, control issues, etc.? If so, what was the most frustrating thing about it?

Did you end the relationship before it had time to do any damage to your self-esteem? Explain.

Have you ever found yourself in a verbally abusive relationship? How did it feel? And how did you manage to break free?

Have you ever dated someone who was dishonest and untruthful? What did it do to the relationship?

What would a pattern of conflict look like in a dating relationship?

How would this look different than having healthy disagreements?

Have you ever dated a "mama's boy," or a "daddy's girl?" How did it impact your relationship?

Would you be able to tell the difference between healthy mood swings and unhealthy ones? Try to describe what each might look like.

Do you agree that sarcasm is just a form of passive-aggressive behavior? How can you tell the difference between healthy teasing between friends and an air of disrespect?

Why would a dysfunctional family be a red flag to watch for when dating? Aren't we all capable of rising above our circumstances?

We've outlined a number of red flags to watch for, but it's not an exhaustive list. What are some other relational red flags to watch for in a dating relationship? List as many as you can.

1.

2.

3.

4.

5.

6.

7.

8.

Do you feel some red flag warnings are more dangerous than others?

List which of the red flags discussed today you would consider "deal breakers" in a dating relationship.

Have you recognized yourself in any of the red flags discussed today? If so, are you willing to list them below?

What should your response be if you feel you have some relational issues that need to be dealt with?

The Right Discussions

1) Read Proverbs 18:14-15. Discuss how this verse might apply to single people in the context of dating and courtship.

2) Have you ever had a "crushed spirit" because of a bad relationship? Ask if anyone would be willing to share their story with the group.

3) Read Proverbs 22:24-25. How can you tell if you are in a relationship with a "hot tempered" person? We all get angry from time to time, so how can you tell the difference between normal anger and a problem with anger?

4) Read Proverbs 25:24. Have you ever tried to navigate a relationship with a quarrelsome person? What was that like? How is that different than having healthy disagreements?

5) Read Luke 6:43-45, and discuss how this verse applies in the context of dating.

6) When choosing a dating partner, what type of "good fruit" should you be watching for in their life and character? Try to list some character qualities you hope to find in a future mate.

The Right Response

In the space below, write out any thoughts or concepts about today's lesson that really spoke to your heart. Have you had a habit of overlooking red flag warnings in the past? Do you see any red flags in your own character that you want God to deal with? Write down anything you think that God is speaking to your spirit, then commit to praying about those things this week.

_____

_____

_____

_____

_____

_____

Session Six

Developing a Spirit of Compatibility

*"I have known many happy marriages, but never a compatible one.
The whole aim of marriage is to fight through and survive the instant
when incompatibility becomes unquestionable."*
- G.K. Chesterton

The Right Approach

Nobody really marries the right person. And no couples are completely compatible from day one. You become right for each other through hard work and patience and a spirit of self-sacrifice. Through developing an attitude of giving instead of demanding. Through learning to compromise, even though you feel like digging in your heels. Through choosing to serve instead of wanting to be served.

The word "compatible" is derived from the words "compassion" and "able." And it is defined as, "capable of existing or living together in harmony." It is the ability to live in compassion with another person. It doesn't mean that you become perfectly in sync, or that you always agree, just that you are capable of overlooking those areas of disagreement and living in harmony in spite of them.

> "If you are a woman of God, don't sell your spiritual birthright by marrying a guy who doesn't deserve you. Your smartest decision in life is to wait for a man who is sold out to Jesus."
>
> – J. Lee Grady

You don't just marry the right person. You must become the right person. And they in turn set out to become the right person for you. That's true for couples who have everything in common, and for couples who have almost nothing in common.

When I (Jimmy) counsel couples, I set out to gauge their level of compatibility, but what I'm really looking for a *spirit of compatibility*. I'm looking for a basic willingness and ability to become compatible. I want to see couples who have a strong desire to overcome the differences between them and create a workable level of compatibility within the relationship.

When looking for the right dating partner, compatibility is one of the most important attributes you should be looking for. But that doesn't necessarily mean you should be looking for sameness or similarity. It isn't important that you find someone who always thinks and acts just as you do. What you're looking for is someone with the ability and willingness to become compatible with you. You are looking for a *spirit of compatibility*.

Gauging Compatibility

Having said that, there is still a good reason that marriage counselors gauge levels of compatibility during counseling. Because relationships are much easier to navigate when couples have a certain degree of parity between them. Differences can be reconciled no matter how great they appear to be, but that doesn't mean couples should overlook differences that could lead to potential problems down the road. Part of assessing compatibility is going into relationships with your eyes wide open. And the best way to do that is to be realistic when looking for a dating partner.

So what are the things you should be looking for when it comes to determining compatibility? Let's look at some of the more basic traits and qualities that I try to assess during pre-marriage counseling.

Healthy Communication Skills

Men and women are inherently different. And we are different in almost every area of life—how we think, how we feel, how we react, how we connect, how we process information, how we grieve, how we compete, how we solve problems, how we see the world around us. We look different. We act different. We *are* different.

And nowhere are we more different than in the way we communicate.

Men tend to communicate in order to relay information. We generally talk more about topics than feelings and emotions. Men are wired to be highly competitive, and tend to focus more on solving problems than discussing them.

Women, on the other hand, communicate in order to connect. They would rather discuss their feelings than things or topics. They are more relational and intuitive, and their speech reflects this truth. Women tend to be more concerned with nurturing people through a crisis than finding a way to solve it.

If you were to walk into a crowded room and announce, "There's a fire on the third floor of this building," the majority of men and women in the room would have very different reactions.

Most of the men would immediately think, *Where is a fire extinguisher? Which way to the nearest stairwell? What is the quickest way to get people off that floor?* Their first instinct would be to solve the problem.

But in that same moment, most women would instinctively think, *Where are my children? How did this happen? I wonder if I know anyone on the third floor? We have to pray that no one gets hurt!* Their initial reaction is rooted in empathy and concern.

> "Allowing each other the freedom to be different is critical to resolving conflict. You not only have to understand your differences, but must try to see things from the other person's perspective."
> - From *The Right One*

We are different because God wired us that way. We are created to complement each other, to bring balance into relationships, to *complete* each other. Successful marriages are not the result of two people who happen to be just like each other. They are the result of two very different individuals who understand their differing views and personalities, and have learned to communicate well enough to work through their differences.

When seeking a potential dating partner, one of the most important areas of compatibility you should be looking for is your ability to communicate effectively as a couple. Are you able to communicate your wants and desires? Do they listen when you talk? Are you able to talk through issues and areas of disagreement in a way that is healthy and non-judgmental? Are you on the same wavelength when navigating basic life issues?

Healthy communication is the bridge that gaps those inherent differences that people bring into a relationship. Without that basic skill, the relationship will always struggle.

Conflict Resolution Skills

Conflict in relationships is not necessarily a bad thing. In fact, healthy conflict is actually a good thing, and can be a sign of strength. Healthy relationships are not those that avoid conflict, but those that learn to effectively resolve conflict when it arises. If couples aren't arguing, they aren't working through their differences. And that only leads to bottled-up anger and resentment.

> "What counts in making a happy marriage is not so much how compatible you are, but how you deal with incompatibility."
>
> – George Levinger

Healthy conflict is the result of two people fully invested in growing a strong and vibrant relationship. When you want a relationship to work, you're willing to do whatever it takes to resolve any hint of discord.

When assessing compatibility with a potential dating partner, don't look for someone who always agrees with you. Look for someone who knows how to have a healthy disagreement. Someone with whom you can communicate well enough to work through any differences between you as they arise.

Shared Vision and Purpose

For relationships to last, they have to be built on a much greater purpose than the happiness and well-being of two single people. And that purpose has to be greater than any amount of stress and struggle that comes into the relationship.

When God brings couples together, he does so with a great deal of intention and vision. He knows why he created each one of us, and what he wants to accomplish in our lives. He gave us specific gifts and talents in order to fulfill that vision. He knows the plans he has for us, and those plans involve marrying the right person.

God also has a vision and purpose for every marriage—something he wants to accomplish in and through the union of every married couple. And it is each couple's responsibility before God to seek out his unique purpose and vision for their marriage.

This is a critical truth to keep in mind when seeking a potential dating partner. It is important that you find someone who shares your basic Christian views and values, so that God can guide and use you as a couple. You want someone who not only shares your faith and priorities, but someone who understands God's ultimate purpose for marriage. Someone who is willing to come alongside you as God molds and shapes your relationship into something he can use for his greater vision.

Ultimately, every marriage must be completely surrendered to God's will and purpose. And the time to surrender your relationship is long before it becomes a potential marriage.

Physical and Emotional Parity

When assessing compatibility with a dating partner, it's also important to be aware of those physical and emotional areas of disparity that could lead to conflict. These are not relational deal-breakers, but they are areas of divergence that are likely to cause strife in ways that you don't always expect.

Couples who come from completely different races, cultures, or ethnic backgrounds will likely face struggles that many other couples won't have to deal with. When you've grown up with vastly different traditions and experiences, you will likely have different expectations and outlooks. Interracial couples may also face prejudices from both inside and outside of their circle of friends and family, and in some cultures, these prejudices run deep.

Couples who come from vastly different socioeconomic circumstances will also face unique struggles. A girl who grew up in a wealthy, privileged family can easily fall for a blue-collar man, but she may have a hard time learning to live on a budget.

Large variances in interests and values can also make relationships difficult to navigate. A health conscious young woman who loves socializing and going to parties may fall for a nerdy guy who would rather spend his time eating chips and playing video games. During the dating phase, these different interests seem intriguing, but in marriage, they can become a huge source of struggle.

Again, these areas of disparity are not necessarily relational deal-breakers, but they are areas of potential conflict that couples need to be aware of before getting into a relationship that may eventually end in marriage.

Compatibility is never innate; it is something that all couples have to work toward. And going into a dating relationship with your eyes wide open is an important first step in the process.

The Right Reading

Jeremiah 29:11; Amos 3:3; Psalm 139:15-16

The Right Questions

In your own words, what does it mean to have a "spirit of compatibility?"

What does it take for married couples to develop compatibility?

If compatibility is something we develop, why is it still important to gauge levels of compatibility before getting into a serious relationship?

Have you experienced firsthand the different ways that men and women have of communicating? Give some specific examples.

Why do you think that men and women are wired so differently?

Why are good communication skills so important to building compatibility between couples?

Give an example of a healthy approach to resolving conflict.

Give an example of an unhealthy approach to resolving conflict.

What would you say are the most important factors or skills in learning to resolve conflict?

Do you agree that God brings couples together for a reason? If so, what are some examples of a specific purpose God might have for a marriage relationship?

Do you believe you've discovered God's purpose for your life? Are you willing to share that with the group?

Do you feel that you know what purpose God might have for your future marriage?

What are some dreams and visions that you hope God will accomplish through your future marriage and family?

Do you agree that couples from different races or cultures might have a harder time in marriage than others? Explain why or why not.

Do you agree that couples from different socioeconomic experiences might have a harder time in marriage than others? Explain why or why not.

Do you know any married couples who came into their relationship with vastly different interests or backgrounds? Was it difficult for them? Explain why or why not.

Describe what you think is the most important trait or skill in developing compatibility in marriage.

The Right Discussion

1) Read Jeremiah 29:11. In what ways should this give you comfort as you navigate your dating relationships? Discuss what this passage means to singles who are looking for a potential marriage partner.

2) What does God expect on our part in order to bring about these future plans that he has for our lives?

3) Read Amos 3:3. What does this passage have to say to singles looking for a dating partner?

4) Discuss the implications of Amos 3:3 for couples who are considering a future marriage. What does it say to couples who have different dreams and visions for their future?

5) Psalm 139:15-16. If God knows our days before any of them come to be, how is it possible for us to make a mistake and marry the wrong person? Discuss what this passage means, and how it applies to dating singles.

The Right Response

In the space below, write out the most important lessons you learned from today's session. Commit to praying about these things over the coming week.

_____

_____

_____

_____

_____

_____

_____

_____

_____

_____

_____

_____

_____

_____

Session Seven
Purposeful Conversations

"Dialogue is to love, what blood is to the body."
- Reuel L. Howe

The Right Approach

When I (Jimmy) counsel engaged couples I always have them complete a *Marriage Expectation Inventory*, which is basically a series of questions aimed at assessing expectations and compatibility.

One young couple brought the forms back, and while going over their answers I noticed a great deal of variance in their answers, which was interesting, since they had been dating for many months.

During the counseling session, I said to the young man, "So, you wrote that you'd like to have six children. Is that right?"

"Absolutely," he answered.

Then I asked the young woman, "And you only want two kids?"

"That's right," she answered.

He looked at her with surprise. "I thought we had talked about this! I've always wanted six children."

Her mouth dropped open. "Not by me!" she told him.

That started an argument that went on for the next half hour, and neither of them seemed willing to bend. It was just one of many differing expectations we uncovered during the session.

This young couple had been dating for almost a year, and had even decided to get married, yet they had never once taken time to talk about the most basic issues of marriage.

> "The single biggest problem in communication is the illusion that it has taken place."
>
> – George Bernard Shaw

They eventually broke off their engagement, which was a good thing, because they appeared to be completely unprepared to build a life together.

You might think that this was an isolated occurrence, but it's actually very common. I see it in my office far too often. Many dating couples are so busy trying to impress each other that they never quite get around to discussing important life issues, like kids, bills, money, careers, and role expectations in the home.

Dating is supposed to be a time of getting to know each other. A time of exploring each other's life goals and purposes, of discovering each other's hopes and expectations for marriage. A time of learning all you can about each other in order to evaluate your level of compatibility for marriage.

But too often it instead becomes an exercise in deceit.

The Purpose of Communication

Conflicting expectations can be a relationship killer, and is likely at the heart of most failed marriages. When couples come into marriage with differing views and goals, they are setting themselves up for a lot of pain and frustration in the future. This doesn't mean that couples have to agree on everything, just that they have a compatible set of intentions and desires for the relationship.

And the only way to know those things is to have a great deal of purposeful and focused conversations while dating. Couples who spend their time talking and exploring and discovering all they can about each other are far more prepared for marriage than those who spend their time smooching, or gazing into each other's eyes for hours on end.

A healthy dating relationship is a communicative one.

So what should dating couples be talking about? The short answer is, "Everything." They should be discussing everything from solving world hunger to setting the table, from politics to green peas, from religion to raking the leaves. No subject should be off limits or too minor to bring up.

When navigating a relationship that may someday lead to marriage, it's impossible to have too much conversation, both meaningful and minute. Because the more you talk, the better you understand what makes each other tick.

Role Expectations

Of all the topics that dating couples should be discussing, role expectations is close to the top of the list. Yet it's one of the most commonly overlooked subjects.

Marriage is a give and take relationship, and there are a lot of details that need to be worked out in order to keep the home running smoothly. These are things that couples should discuss

> "Assumptions are the termites of relationships."
>
> –Henry Winkler

early in their dating relationship, just to make sure they are on the same page.

What is a husband's role in the home? What should the wife's role be? How should chores be divided up? Who should mow the lawn and tend to the garden, and who is responsible for taking care of the home?

These are basic issues in marriage, and the best time to talk them through is long before you reach the stage of exchanging rings.

Children

How many children would you like to have? When would you like to have them? How do you feel they should be raised? Are you a strict disciplinarian, or somewhat permissive? Do you plan to homeschool them? Put them in private school? Public school? What kind of punishment is acceptable—and unacceptable—to you? How do you feel about birth control?

What would happen if you couldn't have children?

These are all critical issues in marriage, and they are important topics to discuss while you are still dating, just to make sure you both have the same expectations.

Finances and Careers

Money is one of the most divisive issues in marriage, and causes more conflict than just about any other issue. It's a subject that few dating couples tend to discuss, because it feels intrusive or meddlesome to bring up. But how you handle money and career decisions will have a tremendous impact on any future marriage, so it needs to be discussed.

If you are a woman, do you plan to work after you get married? Or do you hope to stay home and raise the children? How important is money to you? How important is your career to you? Would you rather be comfortable and live on two incomes, or settle for a smaller house and get by on one? Are you a spender or a saver? Who should handle the finances in the home? What happens in the case of a job loss or financial crisis? Do you cut back on expenses, or both take jobs in order to maintain your lifestyle?

Family Dynamics and Past Relationships

Is your dating partner a "mama's boy" or a "daddy's girl?" Are they close to their family? Or do they feel detached and distant? Did they have a happy childhood, or a dysfunctional one? Have they been married before? Have they ever been in a serious relationship? If so, what caused the breakup? Are they completely over it?

> "Couples who understand the power of words and the dynamics of healthy communication are the ones I know are equipped to build a long and successful marriage relationship."
> - From *The Right One*

We are all affected deeply by our past relationships, whether it is with family, friends, or previous dating partners. And when getting into a dating relationship, it's important to find out all you can about your partner's past and relational history.

Family dysfunctions can easily be passed onto future generations, and can have a marked impact on your future should you decide to become more serious. Ask about past relationships.

Watch how they interact with their parents, siblings, and extended family members. You can learn a lot about someone by simply watching how they treat their friends and family.

Spiritual Practices and Beliefs

There's far more to being a follower of Jesus than going to church. When it comes to choosing a dating partner, spiritual depth and commitment should be at the top of your list of non-negotiables. Because nothing will frustrate a committed follower of Christ more than trying to navigate a relationship with a nominal Christian.

Talk about your spiritual journey, and share your personal testimony with each other. Discuss your beliefs and values, and what you hope God will accomplish in your life and future. Pray together, and talk about what God is teaching you during your times of private devotion. Talk about your spiritual principles and convictions. Are you a charismatic Christian? A cessationist? What does your partner believe about the gifts of the Spirit?

These are all critical issues that need to be discussed when assessing your level of spiritual and emotional compatibility. And the time to discuss them is when deciding whether or not you should get into a serious dating relationship, not when navigating the stress and demands of marriage.

The Right Reading

Genesis 2:24; Ephesians 5:22-28

The Right Questions

Why do you think so many dating couples only talk about superficial things, and not important relational matters?

Has this been true in your own past relationships? Why or why not?

When dating, what is the primary focus among most couples?

Do you agree that dating is too often an "exercise in deceit?" In what ways is that true?

Why is it important to talk about role expectations while dating?

In what ways have role expectations changed over the last few decades?

Have you thought about your own expectations for when you get married? Write out a few of your more important expectations and be ready to share them with the group.

What were the role expectations in your parents' household? And how did this affect your own expectations?

What are some specific role expectations that dating couples should be discussing?

Why is it important to talk about children while dating? Does it feel premature to discuss?

Why is it important to talk about finances and career expectations?

In what ways have career expectations changed over the past few decades?

How important is a healthy family background to you in a dating relationship?

Have you ever dated someone from a dysfunctional family? How did it affect your relationship?

Would you ever consider dating someone who didn't share your spiritual beliefs and practices? Why or why not?

Do you think it's possible to marry a Christian and still be unequally yoked? Explain why or why not.

What are some other things that you think couples need to discuss before deciding to get into a dating relationship?

What would you say are the five most important discussions you need to have with a potential dating partner before taking the relationship further?

The Right Discussion

1) Read Genesis 2:24. What are the physical and spiritual implications of becoming "one flesh" in God's eyes?

2) Discuss what it means when married couples leave their father and mother and "cleave" to each other. How should this affect our expectations of our future marriage?

3) Read Ephesians 5:22-28. What does this passage say about the roles of men and women in marriage? Discuss what it means when it says men are to be the "head" of the wife. Does this imply domination? Or something else?

4) What role do women have in the context of marriage? How would you describe a healthy marriage relationship?

5) When determining roles and expectations in marriage, what does this passage have to say to men? What does it have to say to women?

6) Discuss why it is important to define these expectations before getting into a serious dating relationship.

The Right Response

In the space below, write out what your dream marriage relationship would look like. And be honest and specific. Use this week to pray about your expectations. If any of them are unrealistic, ask God to reveal that to you. If you aren't expecting enough, ask him to reveal that as well.

_____

_____

_____

_____

_____

Session Eight
The Power of Covenant

"Real love, the Bible says, instinctively desires permanence."
- Timothy Keller

The Right Approach

Recent statistics show that about half of all couples decide to live together before marriage. Cohabitation is far more common and accepted than it once was, and has now become common practice, both inside and outside of Christian circles. The reasons couples cohabitate are varied.

Some might be engaged to be married and are living together in order to save expenses while they plan their wedding. Others might be long-time companions who have considered getting married some day, but have just never taken that next step. Still others might be children of divorce who are afraid to get married, because they know how painful a divorce can be. They know in their hearts that it's wrong, but they can't bear the thought of getting into a bad marriage, so they decided instead to simply live together.

As a pastor, I (Jimmy) increasingly see cohabitating couples in our church services, and many of them are people who have grown up in the church. They know what the Bible has to say about sex before marriage, but they willfully choose to disobey. Either they think the practice of marriage is outdated, or they know that they are in the wrong but just don't care.

Others may not have grown up in the church, so they don't really understand the biblical view on the subject. Many of their friends live together, so they see nothing wrong with the lifestyle. In those cases it's my job as a pastor to teach them.

The reality is, God does not take cohabitation lightly. He created marriage for a reason, and he longs to see couples enter into a lifelong covenantal relationship. But "shacking up" is not what he intended. In fact, cohabitation is in direct opposition to God's will and intent for mankind, and a direct offense to God's holiness and character.

> "Marriage is deeply satisfying, incredibly fulfilling and loads of fun. It makes the harsh edges of life a little softer. It brings joy and hope and laughter. But it's not easy, and it's not something to rush into without thinking."
>
> – Jason Boyett

Why Marriage?

Many cohabitating couples say that in God's eyes, they are married. *If we love each other, and are committed to the relationship, isn't that the same thing as marriage? Why is a piece of paper so important?*

On the surface it may seem like a logical argument, but the reality is, cohabitating is the opposite of commitment. That's why it is not recognized as a legal marriage—by the government, the church, or by God. The primary intent of living together is to avoid the commitment of marriage. When you are living together, you can leave at any time without consequence. And so can your partner. You are not bound by law, nor any other entity. And in God's eyes, you are not married, no matter how committed or loving you feel, because you haven't entered into the covenantal bond of marriage.

Cohabitation is a living arrangement, not a covenant. And there is a very big difference.

Why Covenant?

God is a covenantal God. Covenant is how he chooses to communicate with us. He redeemed us through covenant, and guaranteed us eternal life through the covenantal blood of Jesus.

The Bible is a covenantal document, made up of the Old and New Testaments. And the word "testament" in Latin is "Covenant." The word covenant means "to cut." You don't *make* a covenant; you "cut covenant."

The first marriage between Adam and Eve was described in the second chapter of Genesis when God "cut" Adam and took a rib from his side to create his wife, Eve. The New Covenant of salvation came when Jesus was crucified on the cross, and bled to pay for our sins. Covenant demands sacrifice and permanence.

God deals with man through covenant, because covenant is the language of God's heart. God is about permanence and commitment. He brings us into relationship with himself through covenant, and he binds our hearts together in marriage through covenant with each other.

> "Every relationship for a Christian is an opportunity to love another person like God has loved us."
>
> –Joshua Harris

A wedding is a covenantal ceremony. It is our way of acknowledging our commitment to both God and society, and of binding ourselves to each other, legally, spiritually, and physically. It is far more than a piece of paper.

There is no room in God's paradigm for "shacking up," or living together, or "cohabitating." These things are a direct affront to God, because they all shake their fist at covenant. Sex before marriage is wrong because it is sex without the blessing and commitment of covenant.

In God's economy, without covenant there is no relationship, only a pattern of willful disobedience and sin.

The Power of Covenant

The question many of us have is, if cohabitation is wrong, and most couples know that, why is it so prevalent? Why are so many couples living in disobedience to God's will?

Though there are likely many reasons for the trend, I believe that at the heart of the cohabitation movement is a basic fear of marriage. People have seen so many marriages end in divorce over the last few decades, and couples are simply afraid to commit. *What if we get married and it doesn't work out?* they think. So they decide instead to live together, just to test the relationship out before committing.

It is a movement driven by fear, and riddled with insecurity and doubt.

It's not hard to understand the concern. The institution of marriage has taken a beating over the last few years, and it's no surprise that many have lost faith in the idea.

If you are single, and have found yourself avoiding relationships out of a basic fear of marriage, let me calm your spirit. Marriage was created by God, and God will sustain his creation, no matter how assaulted and battered it becomes. Marriage is not some invention of the courts, or an institution implemented by man. It was set in place by God at the beginning of creation, and he has no intention of letting man destroy it.

> "A successful marriage requires falling in love many times, always with the same person."
>
> – Mignon McLaughlin

Marriage is a covenantal commitment, and God never turns his back on covenant. When two people stand before God, family, and friends, pledging to stay together through thick and thin, no matter what hardship comes their way, God takes notice. And God blesses the relationship in ways that you and I can't fathom.

The blessings of a covenantal marriage are both immense and eternal. There is nothing on earth more intimately rewarding and satisfying than a truly great marriage. And with the right attitude, it's a blessing that any couple can experience firsthand!

Don't let your fear of commitment cause you to miss out on God's most powerful blessing to mankind. When you find *The Right One*, allow God to bless and guide your relationship. And when the time comes, seal your commitment in the covenantal bond of marriage. Then lean on God and trust him to get you through any trial or struggle that comes your way.

With God's help, every marriage has a 100% chance of success! So let your relationships be rooted in faith, not fear.

The Right Reading

1 Corinthians 7:2; Ephesians 5:31-32

The Right Questions

Why do you think cohabitation has become so commonplace today?

Have you noticed that same trend among your Christian friends and relatives? Why do you think that's true?

What would you say to somehow who claims that marriage is obsolete and old-fashioned?

Do you agree that cohabitation is not the same as marriage in the eyes of God? Why or why not?

Describe why cohabitation is an assault on God's holiness and character.

What would you say is the primary reason couples decide to live together instead of getting married?

How would you describe the difference between a commitment and a covenant?

Why is the shedding of blood a symbol of covenant?

In what way is Jesus' sacrifice on the cross a symbol of our covenantal sacrifice in marriage?

Do you know any people who cohabitate because they are afraid of commitment? What would you say to them about their fears?

Do you find yourself pushing people away because you fear commitment deep in your heart?

In what ways does God bless couples who choose to enter into the covenant of marriage instead of cohabitating?

What would you say to couples who are cohabitating because they are afraid of what might happen if they chose to get married?

If you could sum up today's lesson in one sentence, what would it be?

The Right Discussion

1) Read 1 Corinthians 7:1-2. What does this passage say to those who might believe that cohabitation is acceptable to God as long as they are committed to each other?

2) Can you think of any passages in Scripture that imply an acceptance of sex outside of marriage?

3) If sex outside of marriage is always wrong, yet has been become accepted both inside and outside of Christian circles, what should the church do to help reverse this trend?

4) Read Ephesians 5:31-32. Discuss what Paul means when he calls marriage a "profound mystery."

5) In what way is the covenant of marriage an archetype of Christ and the church?

6) Discuss why single people should not be afraid to commit to marriage when they find the right marriage partner.

7) What are some of the ways that God works to help couples keep their covenant with each other in marriage?

The Right Response

In the space below, write three of the most profound thoughts or lessons you've learned during the course of this study. In what ways has this series of lessons better prepared you to find the right marriage partner some day? Is there anything you've been doing that you hope to change? This week, commit to praying that God would guide you in your future relationships as you put your future completely in his hands. Commit to moving forward in faith, not fear, and trusting that God's timing is perfect.

_____

_____

_____

_____

_____

_____

_____

_____

Suggestions for Leaders

Leading a Bible study can feel like a daunting experience, but it's actually not that difficult—especially if it's a discussion format study. This particular series is designed to be an interactive conversation, not a class lecture. When leading the group, begin by seeing yourself as more of a facilitator than a teacher.

Here are a few suggestions to get you started, and to help things go more smoothly:

Preparing the Lesson

Begin by praying that God would guide you as you prepare to facilitate the lesson.

As you prepare for your lesson, make sure you have answered all the questions thoroughly, just as you would if you were attending the group.

After answering all the questions, go back and earmark those questions that you hope will lead to the most lively and engaging conversations. This will help you remember any important points you hope to bring up.

Whenever possible, think of a personal story or anecdote to share in order to keep the conversation flowing. Make notes of those stories to help you remember.

While preparing to facilitate, try to identify two or three "big ideas" from each session that you hope the group will take away from the lesson. Note those in the margins so that you can highlight those particular points during the lesson.

Remember that these lessons are designed to comfortably fill a 60- to 90-minute discussion format, so if your class is shorter or longer than that, you may need to cut a few questions, or add a few of your own.

Once you've prepared your lesson, cover the study in prayer. Pray that God would lead your thoughts and heart as you facilitate the lesson, and pray individually for each person in the group. Ask God to speak specifically to each person in the class.

Leading the Group

Remember to start and end on time. Lessons that run too long can easily drift off course. So keep the class focused, and keep your eye on the clock.

At the beginning of each class, remind the members of your group that this is a discussion class, and not a lecture. Encourage everyone to participate.

Don't be afraid of silence. Sometimes people need time to process their thoughts, and if you always chime in and rescue the class, some might be less likely to participate.

Avoid answering your own questions. If you don't get a response, try restating the question in a different way.

Encourage more than one answer to each question. Once someone has answered, you might say, "That's a good answer. What do the rest of you think?" or "Does anyone else have any thoughts?"

Whenever possible, encourage members to share their personal stories or testimonies.

Learn to recognize rabbit trails, and quickly head them off before they take the discussion off-topic.

Never cut someone off in mid-answer. If people think you are starting to take over the group, they will shut down and stop responding.

Always end your lessons in a time of prayer. It's best to have members of the group pray instead of doing it yourself.

Lesson Format

The Right Approach

Each lesson in the series begins with a short story or essay that sets up the day's topic. We call it "The Right Approach" because it introduces the central theme of the day's lesson. This section is designed to be read by each member during the previous week. You might begin each lesson by asking, "Did everyone have time to read through today's lesson?"

You may also decide to begin each class by reading this section aloud (or designating someone in the group to read it), since this section sets up many of the questions to follow.

A good way to begin each lesson is to ask if anyone has any thoughts or comments on the lesson before you get started. But don't allow too much discussion at this point, since you don't want to get ahead of the lesson.

The Right Reading

This second section lists the Bible versus that we will be discussing in the day's lesson. We suggest that you have someone read these passages aloud at the beginning of each session, then have someone open in a word of prayer.

Since we will be discussing these verses during the course of the study, it might be better to not elaborate on them until later in the study. Simply encourage members to keep these passages in mind as you begin the lesson.

The Right Questions

This section is the heart of the study. The questions are designed to be answered by each member during the previous week, so you might begin by asking if everyone had time to do that. Members should still be able to benefit from the study, even if they haven't done their homework, but discussions will be much more engaging if everyone comes prepared. It might be a good idea to remind the group each week to do that if at all possible.

As the group leader, we suggest that you be the one to read these questions aloud, instead of having members of the group take turns reading them. This establishes you as the leader, and also allows you to rephrase each question in your own words when needed.

Remember that some questions can be answered rather quickly, while others might take a little time to process. So don't be afraid to pace yourself, and allow each question to be thoroughly explored before moving forward.

When appropriate, allow the discussion to sidetrack a bit. If someone has a good thought or follow up question, let the discussion flow that direction. Some rabbit trails might be worth following. Just be prepared to bring the discussion back on topic when the time comes.

The Right Discussion

This section is designed to show members how each lesson is rooted in Scripture and biblical teaching. This is where you will be re-reading the day's passages one at a time and exploring them deeper. Make sure that everyone has their Bible open, so that they can follow along as the passages are read.

This is also a good opportunity to ask if anyone knows any other passages or stories from the Bible that might add to the lesson.

The Right Response

This last section is intended as a way to conclude your lesson. Read this section aloud, and then give everyone a few minutes to write their responses in the space provided. Before ending in prayer, ask if anyone has any specific thoughts or prayer requests they'd like to share with the group.

Remember to end each lesson encouraging members to pray during the coming week for wisdom and guidance as God continues to speak to them through the course of this study.

Endnotes

1. "Sexual Atheism: Christian Dating Data Reveals a Deeper Spiritual Malaise," by Kenny Luck, www.charismamag.com, 4/8/2014.

Pre-Marriage Inventory

Discussing Personal Issues, Expectations and Role Concepts
by Jimmy Evans

One of the most important issues in being happily married is to be in agreement on essential issues. The purpose of this inventory is to make sure all important issues have been discussed and agreed upon before marriage. It is much easier to work through issues before marriage. Also, it is important to know if you cannot agree on an issue or issues. If you cannot, you need to seriously consider the ramifications. Is it a deal breaker? Is it important or relatively unimportant? Can you live the rest of your life not being in agreement? How will this affect your children? Think long-term.

The best way to use this inventory is for each person to complete it separately. Once both of you have finished answering your inventory you then discuss each answer. If there is a pre-marriage counselor involved hand your completed inventory to him or her without showing your fiancée your answers. The counselor will then have a session with you and discuss your answers and help you reach agreement if necessary.

If you do not have a pre-marriage counselor, complete your inventory separately and then plan a time to talk through it. You need to have at least a couple of hours or more to make sure you aren't rushed. If you reach an impasse and cannot agree you need to consider getting help from a Christian counselor, pastor or trusted person who is qualified.

It is common for couples to disagree when answering this inventory honestly. In fact, it surprises a lot of couples to know they were in disagreement and didn't know it. That is the importance of this exercise. It causes you to talk about things you might not have discussed until you were married and began to fight. The process of taking a few hours to complete this inventory and discussing your answers with your fiancée will be well worth it.

After completing your inventory and as you are comparing your answers you can refer to my comments on each question online at www.marriagetoday.com/premarriageinventory

Communication

a. Is there an issue you haven't discussed with your fiancée that you feel needs to be discussed before you marry?

b. Is there an issue or issues you are afraid to talk about for fear it will endanger your relationship?

c. Do you feel free to be honest with your fiancée?

d. Do you currently feel as though you have satisfactory communication in your relationship? If not, how could it be improved?

e. Do you feel as though you or your fiancée has anger or dominance issues that need to be addressed? Does the fear of making your fiancée angry keep you from communicating with them?

f. Do you feel as though your fiancée respects your opinion?

g. How much time a day do you believe it takes to properly communicate once you are married?

h. How healthy was the communication in the family you grew up in? If it was unhealthy, what will you do to make sure you won't practice the same things in your new family?

i. How important is it to you that problems are resolved daily and you don't go to bed angry?

Roles

a. Who will manage the money?

b. Will the wife work outside of the home?

c. Who is primarily responsible for disciplining the children?

d. Is it ok for a wife to initiate sex?

e. Who will cook and clean the house?

f. Who will take care of the yard and overall maintenance?

g. Who will empty the trash?

h. Who is the head of the home or will you be equals?

g. Are the basic needs of men and women in marriage the same or are they different? What happens when your spouse wants you to meet a need for them that you don't have?

Children

a. How many children will you have?

b. Will you spank them? How will you discipline them?

c. In what church or type of church will you raise them?

d. What type of school will your children attend?

e. How important will college and higher education be for your children?

f. How important will spirituality and Christ be in raising them?

g. If you have a blended family, will you share in the parenting responsibilities with your spouse?

h. If you have a blended family, will you share all decision-making concerning your biological children with your spouse?

Sex

a. Is there anything important about your sexual history you haven't discussed with your fiancée?

b. Do you have any sexual, emotional or physical problems that could have a negative effect on you or your sex life once married?

c. Where have you gotten most of your information about sex?

d. What is the main difference between men and women sexually?

e. How often will you have sex? What is too little and what it too much?

f. What happens when your spouse wants sex and you don't?

e. How important is it to you that your spouse cares for their health and appearance? Do you have any concerns?

f. Do you agree with what the Bible has to say about sex? Is there anything you don't agree with?

g. Are you embarrassed to talk about sex? If so, do you believe that will have a negative influence on your marriage?

h. Is there anything about men or women you don't understand related to sex but want to?

Finances

a. Who will be primarily responsible to make money -- you, your spouse or both of you?

b. How important is financial status to you?

c. How much money can you spend without your spouses input?

d. How will you make important financial decisions?

e. Do you feel as though your spouse sees money the same as you?

f. Do you believe debt is wrong? How much debt should you have?

g. How important is saving money in your marriage? What percentage of your income should be saved?

h. How important is tithing (giving 10% of your income to your church) and giving offerings to ministries?

i. What is your main financial concern after you are married?

Spirituality

a. How important is it to you that you have a spiritual marriage and family?

b. How often do you want to pray with your spouse?

c. Do you have a basic agreement about the Bible?

d. Will you follow the Bible's teachings in establishing the practices of your home and in your decision-making?

e. Who will teach your children about God and how important is that to you?

f. How important is it to you that your spouse has a daily time of praying and reading the Bible? How much of a difference do you think it makes in your marriage?

In-Laws

a. What do you think about your fiancées parents?

b. Is there anything about your future in-laws that concerns you but you haven't discussed with your fiancée?

c. Will you allow your parents and in-laws to babysit your children?

d. How much time will you spend with your in-laws?

e. How much time do you want to spend as a couple with your parents?

f. How much control do you feel your parents and your future in-laws have over your relationship? Are you concerned about either of them trying to control you?

g. What will you do if your parents try to control you or your marriage?

h. What will you do if your parents criticize your spouse?

i. Will you tell your parents about problems you are having in your marriage?

j. Who will you spend the holidays with? How will you decide who to be with?

www.ingramcontent.com/pod-product-compliance
Lightning Source LLC
Chambersburg PA
CBHW081250040426

42452CB00015B/2777